Magical Puzzles

Enchanted Puzzles

Written by
Samantha Williams

Illustrated by
Samantha Loman

WINDMILL
BOOKS

Published in 2020 by **Windmill Books**, an imprint of Rosen Publishing
29 East 21st Street, New York, NY 10010

Illustrated by Samantha Loman
Written by Samantha Williams
Edited by Susannah Bailey
Designed by Well Nice Ltd

Cataloging-in-Publication Data

Names: Williams, Samantha. | Loman, Sam.
Title: Enchanted puzzles / Samantha Williams, illustrated by Sam Loman.
Description: New York : Windmill Books, 2020. | Series: Magical puzzles
Identifiers: ISBN 9781538391723 (pbk.) | ISBN 9781538391747 (library bound) | ISBN 9781538391730 (6 pack)
Subjects: LCSH: Picture puzzles--Juvenile literature. | Fantasy--Juvenile literature.
Classification: LCC GV1507.P47 W55 2020 | DDC 793.73--dc23

Manufactured in the United States of America

CPSIA Compliance Information: Batch #BS19WM:
For Further Information contact Rosen Publishing, New York, New York at 1-800-237-9932

Contents

Festive Fun	4	Time for Bed	17
Awesome Ice	5	Super Sweet	18
Twinkly Tiaras	6	Home Time!	19
Finders Keepers	7	Friends Forever	20
Fairy Picnic	8	Precious Pet	21
Stunning Sandcastle	9	Forest Friends	22
Sort It Out	10	Beautiful Hair	23
Remember, Remember	11	Otter Spotter	24
Lost and Found	13	Super Search	25
Magical Trail	14	Magical Mix-Up	26
Pool Party	15	Make a Splash!	27
Gem-tastic	16	Mirror, Mirror	28
		Find the Flowers	29
		Answers	30

Festive Fun

It's Christmas, and Santa Claus has left presents! Can you find where all 11 of them are?

Awesome Ice

The unicorns are using their horns to make ice sculptures, but one sculpture has been made with a difference. Can you discover what it is?

Twinkly Tiaras

Which two beautiful tiaras are exactly the same?

Finders Keepers

Lots of pretty keys have sunk to the bottom of the ocean over the years!
Link each one to its pair, and find one that doesn't have a match.

Fairy Picnic

Princess Poppy has made a list of all the things she wants at her birthday picnic.
Can you find all the words in the grid below?

I	C	E	C	R	E	A	M	A	M	A	S
C	L	E	M	O	N	A	D	E	A
R	C	S	K	L	E	M	H	A	N
E	G	R	A	N	M	C	A	K	E
C	C	R	S	A	I	A	P	P	W
I	H	S	A	W	P	N	P	A	I
U	O	A	D	P	R	P	E	K	C
J	C	N	R	D	E	R	L	D	H
C	A	E	P	R	M	S	S	E	E
S	N	O	O	R	A	C	A	M	S

GRAPES

JUICE

ICE CREAM

APPLES

SANDWICHES

LEMONADE

CAKE

MACAROONS

8

Stunning Sandcastle

On a clean piece of paper, copy these sandcastles. Then decorate the mermaids' home with drawings of pretty shells and sea creatures.

Sort It Out

What a mess! Can you help Little Squirt figure out which of the anchors is attached to each boat?

A

B

C

1

2

3

Remember, Remember

Take a good look at this scene, remembering as much as you can.
Then turn the page and test your memory!

Remember, Remember

Can you remember what you saw? Write down
everything you can on a separate piece of paper!

1. Which animal was in the tree?

....

2. How many mermaids were swimming?

....

3. Which two of these butterflies did you see?

A   B   C

4. Which creature is sitting on a mermaid's lap?

....

5. What do the toadstools look like?

A   B   C

6. Who is flying in the sky?

....

7. Which of these mermaids has her hands in her hair?

A   B   C

8. Are the rabbits white or brown?

....

Lost and Found

Which of the treasure chests is the one the prince is looking for? Use the clues to figure it out.

It has a lock on it.

It has a flat lid.

It has handles.

It contains a golden goblet.

Magical Trail

Can you find all these magical words in the grid below?
Words are spelled out forward, backward, and diagonally.

MERMAID UNICORN SHIMMER FAIRY

SPARKLE WAND RAINBOW WINGS

M	E	R	W	I	N	R	G	H	W
E	U	S	P	A	R	K	L	E	I
D	S	N	D	R	W	I	N	G	S
I	F	A	I	R	Y	D	A	I	R
A	A	W	U	C	W	A	N	B	A
M	E	N	N	S	O	B	O	A	I
R	I	N	I	H	W	R	D	S	W
E	S	R	C	F	A	I	N	H	W
M	P	R	E	M	M	I	H	S	A
A	R	A	I	N	B	O	W	I	N

Pool Party

Which inflatable flamingo float looks different from the rest? And which watermelon float has a different number of seeds?

Gem-tastic

Look carefully in the large grid to find this pattern of gems there.

Time for Bed

Can you spot six differences between these two pictures?

Super Sweet

Look carefully for these yummy treats!

CUPCAKE	CANDY	COOKIE	CHOCOLATE
DOUGHNUT	MANGO	CHERRY	LOLLIPOP

C	P	O	P	I	L	L	O	L	S
C	H	C	C	O	O	K	I	E	R
H	S	O	A	C	A	N	D	L	T
E	P	P	C	O	G	N	A	M	U
R	R	C	R	O	Y	L	C	H	N
R	I	H	R	D	L	O	A	Y	H
Y	B	R	N	L	T	A	N	R	G
I	E	A	L	L	O	Y	T	R	U
B	C	H	O	C	O	L	L	E	O
S	S	C	U	P	C	A	K	E	C	D

Home Time!

Can you help Sparklebreeze reach her castle?
Use your finger to trace a path through the maze.

Finish

Start

Friends Forever

Invent cute names for all of these fairy pairs,
then write them on a separate piece
of paper.

....

....

....

....

....

....

....

....

....

....

....

Precious Pet

Sparkle can't find her pet kitten, Cloudpuff!
Can you see where she is hiding?

21

Forest Friends

Put this picture of Harvest and her woodland creatures back together! Can you spot which piece doesn't fit anywhere?

A

B

C

D

E

F

G

Beautiful Hair

Copy these fancy unicorns onto a piece of paper, then use your best markers to add long, magnificent manes and tails. Let your imagination go wild, and add as many ribbons and bows as you like!

Otter Spotter

Can you find this adorable baby otter in the crowd?

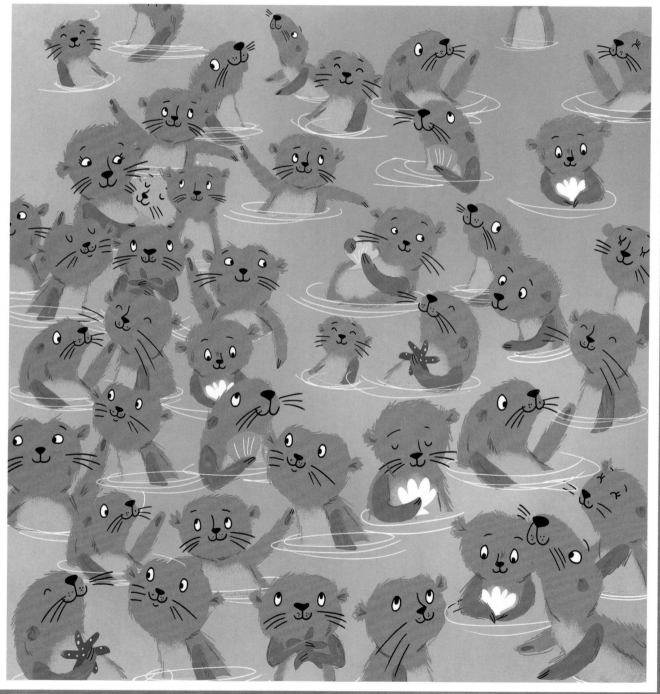

Super Search

Look for all the mermaids' magical friends hidden in this word search grid. Words can be found forward, backward, and diagonally.

P	T	N	A	I	G	O	N
I	C	G	C	E	N	R	O
X	G	E	R	F	F	O	G
I	I	N	N	I	L	G	A
E	A	I	E	T	A	E	R
U	N	E	L	N	A	N	D
N	F	A	I	R	Y	U	N
U	N	I	C	O	R	N	R

PIXIE

FAIRY

ELF

GIANT

DRAGON

CENTAUR

UNICORN

GENIE

Magical Mix-Up

The unicorns and fairies have been to the fair. They have each won a balloon, but their strings are in a tangle! Can you see which balloon belongs to which pair?

Make a Splash!

The mermaids are playing water volleyball, while the unicorns and fairies cheer them on.
Can you fit the circles into the scene? Which of the circles cannot be placed?

Mirror, Mirror

These gorgeous mer-mirrors have all been found in the sand. They seem the same, but one of them is slightly different. Can you find it?

Find the Flowers

There are so many beautiful flowers in the unicorns' magical land. Can you find all of their names hidden in the grid?

ROSE   LILY   SUNFLOWER   LILAC

IRIS   DAISY   TULIP   ORCHID

L	U	N	F	L	O	L	I	S	Y
I	T	U	L	I	P	U	L	I	O
C	R	O	D	P	L	I	Y	T	R
A	R	E	C	A	U	N	O	R	C
L	D	S	I	S	I	R	I	A	H
I	L	O	L	T	I	S	N	R	I
L	T	R	O	P	Y	D	Y	F	D
S	U	N	F	L	O	W	E	R	L
O	W	E	I	I	S	U	N	L	H
R	O	L	A	F	E	L	D	A	C

Answers

Page 4: Festive Fun

Page 5: Awesome Ice

Page 6: Twinkly Tiaras

Page 7: Finders Keepers

Page 8: Fairy Picnic

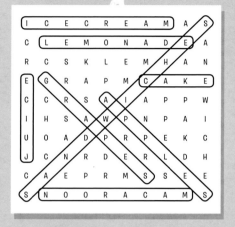

Page 10: Sort It Out

A 3
B 2
C 1

Page 11: Remember, Remember

1 Squirrels
2 2
3 A, C
4 A bird
5 A
6 Fairies
7 C
8 White

Page 14: Magical Trail

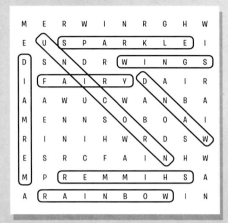

```
M E R W I N R G H W
E U S P A R K L E I
D S N D R W I N G S
I F A I R Y D A I R
A A W U C W A N B A
M E N N S O B O A I
R I N I H W R D S W
E S R C F A I N H W
M P R E M M I H S A
A R A I N B O W I N
```

Page 16: Gem-tastic

Page 18: Super Sweet

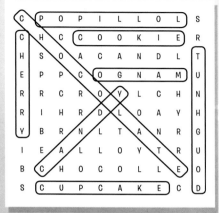

```
C P O P I L L O L S
C H C C O O K I E R
H S O A C A N D L T
E P P C O G N A M U
R R C R O Y L C H N
R I H R D L O A Y H
Y B R N L T A N R G
I E A L L O Y T R U
B C H O C O L L E O
S C U P C A K E C C
```

Page 15: Pool Party

Page 17: Time for Bed

Page 19: Home Time!

Page 21: Precious Pet

Page 22: Forest Friends

Piece D doesn't fit anywhere.

Page 24: Otter Spotter

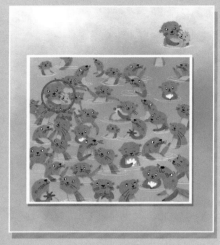

Page 25: Super Search

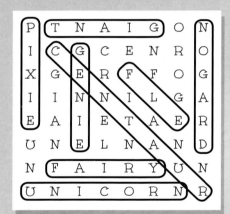

Page 26: Magical Mix-Up

1 D
2 B
3 C
4 A

Page 27: Make a Splash!

Circle C cannot be placed.

Page 28: Mirror, Mirror

C

Page 29: Find the Flowers

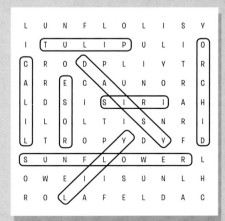